# 40 OLD TESTAMENT
## BIBLE STORIES

## ANDY ROBB

Text © Andy Robb 2018
Illustrations © Walk Through the Bible 2018
Published 2018 by CWR, Waverley Abbey House, Waverley Lane, Farnham, Surrey GU9 8EP, UK. CWR is a Registered Charity – Number 294387 and a Limited Company registered in England – Registration Number 1990308.
The right of Andy Robb to be identified as the author and illustrator of this work has been asserted by him in accordance with the Copyright, Designs and Patents Act 1988.
Text taken from various titles in the '50s' Bible story series by Andy Robb, published by CWR.
For a list of National Distributors, visit cwr.org.uk/distributors
Concept development, editing, design and production by CWR with Walk Through the Bible.
Printed in the UK by Linney

# CONTENTS

# MIRACLE MAKER

It's one thing to create something if you've got the stuff to make it with, but imagine making a clay pot without any clay or baking a cake without any ingredients. That would be weird, wouldn't it? It would also be impossible – but not for someone like God.

When God made the universe (including planet Earth and everything on it), guess what He had to make it with? You're right! Nothing. Zilch! The Bible says that before the universe was made there was just God. That was it. Nothing else, just Him.

For starters, at the very beginning it was pitch black. If people had been around (which they weren't) they wouldn't have been able to see their hands in front of their faces. So how did God create light? Simple. He commanded it to come into being. In fact, that's how everything was created – by God telling it to exist.

When God made the world, it was completely covered in water until He made the water separate to make way for some nice dry land. God filled the earth with all sorts of plants and animals. He put the sun in just the right place in outer space so nothing gets either fried or frozen and He even made the moon to be the most amazing night-light. How considerate is that?!

You're probably thinking that it must have taken God yonks to make everything, but think again! Head for Bible book Genesis, chapter 2 and verses 1 to 3.

# GARDEN GATE GUARD

I don't know if you've got a garden or not but most garden owners have some sort of gate to stop people walking in and trampling all over their nice, pretty flower beds or nicking the produce from their vegetable patch. But did you know that the world's very first people (Adam and Eve) had a garden? Yep, they did. Just in case you run away with the idea that it had a neat lawn and a stone path leading up to a shed then let me put you straight.

Their garden was the most wonderful, exotic paradise you could ever imagine and four rivers flowed out from it in different directions. Slap-bang in the middle of the garden stood a couple of rather important trees that had been put there by God. Well, actually God had put all the trees there (because He had made the world) but these particular trees were there for a special reason. One of the trees gave life and God had given Adam and Eve the thumbs-up to eat its fruit. The other tree gave the power to know the difference between right and wrong but this one was well and truly off-limits. Take a munch from the fruit of this tree and they were doomed to die. Why spoil things by disobeying God? It was a no-brainer... or so you'd have thought.

Just when everything in the garden was looking rosy, along came someone to put a spanner in the works. It was none other than God's enemy (the devil) masquerading as a sneaky serpent. He'd come to trick the perfect pair into throwing their good life away in a moment of madness. The serpent quickly persuaded them that they'd maybe got the story wrong and that they wouldn't really die if they snacked on some of the forbidden fruit. What could possibly be the harm in just a teensy nibble of the juicy fruit?

So that's exactly what Adam and Eve did. No prizes for guessing that they were rumbled by God. He knew full well that they'd disobeyed Him and now it was time for the consequences. Did God make them mow the lawn or pick up all the leaves as a punishment? Nope, far worse.

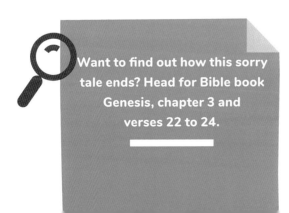

Want to find out how this sorry tale ends? Head for Bible book Genesis, chapter 3 and verses 22 to 24.

# RAINBOW REMINDER

Way back in the mists of time there was a whopping big flood that just about destroyed everything on the planet.

Here's what happened.

When God created human beings, He was pleased with the way they'd turned out, but it didn't take long for our distant ancestors to turn their backs on Him and to go their own wicked way. This upset God big time.

There was one guy though who hadn't gone the way of all the others. His name was Noah and he lived a life that pleased God – so much so that God decided that, although He was going to wipe everyone else off the face of the earth because of their wickedness, Noah and his family would be spared. That was a bit jammy for them, wasn't it? Bet they were grateful for a godly dad!

God told Noah to build a huge box-shaped boat (called an ark), big enough not only to hold his family, but also two of every kind of animal that roamed the earth and soared in the skies. When God's worldwide flood came everyone on the ark would be safe.

Sure enough what God promised came to pass and a mahoosive flood (the like of which had never happened before) engulfed the entire planet, destroying every land-based creature that wasn't afloat on Noah's ark.

When the flood waters eventually subsided and the ark had come to rest, Noah and his family went out to survey the damage. They were the only survivors and, along with their animal passengers, it was up to them to set about re-populating the world.

But hang on a minute. Supposing the same thing happened again and Noah's descendants also did the dirty on God? Would God bring another flood?

He'd already made His mind up on the matter.

The Bible says that God promised Noah that the world would never again suffer a destructive flood like they'd just lived through. Yes, there might be local floods because that's what storms do, but never a worldwide one to wipe away wickedness.

To prove that He was going to be true to His Word, God said that He was going to give people a sign.

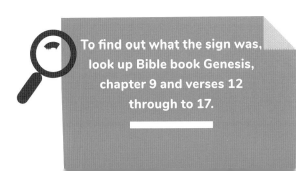

To find out what the sign was, look up Bible book Genesis, chapter 9 and verses 12 through to 17.

# TOWER POWER

Once the world's biggest flood had subsided, God told Noah and his family to have loads of kids and to fill the world with people again. So far, so good. Over time the earth's population grew and grew and then, just when it looked like everything was going to plan, a bunch of them decided to be awkward and do their own thing.

Noah's descendants had been gradually heading away from where the ark had parked up (on Mount Ararat) in search of new land, but when they came to a flat bit of land in Babylonia, everyone downed luggage and came to an abrupt halt. They'd had enough of this living out of a suitcase lark.

Time to settle down and build proper houses for themselves. Nothing wrong with that, you may think. Let's see what else they had to say for themselves. 'How about we build a whopping big tower that reaches up to heaven to show how great we are?' The thinking was that if they made a bit of a name for themselves, they'd be set up for life and could stay put in Babylonia. No more of this 'filling the earth' stuff that God had told 'em to do. Who wants to keep moving around to new places when a comfortable life in Babylonia beckons?

God was having none of it. People who did as they pleased rather than obeying Him was the reason why He'd wiped them off the face of the earth in the first place. God had to do something before the rot set in again. Up until that point in history, everybody spoke the same language, but not for long. While the settlers were busy building their tower, God came down and put an end to their nonsense in an instant.

Check out what God did in Bible book Genesis, chapter 11 and verses 7 to 9.

# STAR TREK

Abram (later called Abraham) lived in Ur. His ancestors had settled there after coming off Noah's ark. Ur was a prosperous city and by all accounts Abram was a wealthy chap in his own right. Just when it looked like Abram could settle down to a nice, comfy life, his dad (Terah) decided to move the family to a place called Canaan (over 1,000 miles away!). Terah never actually made it that far. He stopped off along the way at Haran, where he eventually died.

When Abram was 75 years old, God turned up with a bit of news. He wanted Abram to up sticks and leave Haran and to head off in the direction of Canaan to finish the journey his dad had started. In those days you couldn't just hop on a plane and arrive at your destination a few hours later ('cos planes hadn't been invented yet). There was nothing for it but to load up your camels and travel the hard way, by foot.

You're probably wondering why on earth God would ask an old man to make such a mahoosive journey, so I'll tell you. God was gonna start a brand-new nation of people who worshipped Him and who would gradually get to know Him. Abram was God's main man to get it all up and running, and is one of the stars of the Bible. But first the nation needed a bit of land to call their own, and that's what Canaan was going to be. Just in case you were worried that he'd get lonely all on his lonesome, let me put your mind at rest. Abram also took with him his wife Sarai, his nephew Lot and all his possessions and servants.

God also told him he would have loads and loads and loads of children!

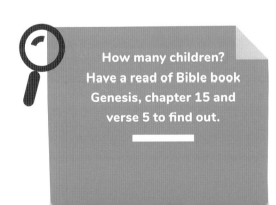

How many children? Have a read of Bible book Genesis, chapter 15 and verse 5 to find out.

# BONKERS BOMBSHELL!

Here's a question for you. If God turned up at your house, would you recognise Him? That was Abraham's dilemma. One day, as he sheltered from the sweltering heat at the entrance to his tent, three men showed up. I can only guess that Abraham knew that there was something pretty special about these guys because the Bible tells us that he bowed down with his face in the dirt.

Abraham insisted that the three of them stay for a bite to eat and a refreshing drink. The guests took him up on his offer and Sarah (Abraham's wife) set about rustling up a tasty meal for them.

The three mysterious visitors obviously weren't in a rush because the Bible helpfully informs us that Sarah had time to bake some fresh bread, which would no doubt have taken quite a while! Added to which she didn't give them just a sandwich but pulled out all the stops and cooked a calf from the herd to set it before them.

Now for the bombshell. One of the visitors just about blew Abraham away with the awesome news that Sarah would give birth to a son in nine months' time. *What!?* *That's impossible*, thought Abraham. He and his good lady wife were well past it (sorry to be so rude) and having a kid at their ripe old age was a ridiculous notion. Sarah was ear-wigging at the tent door and overheard what was said. She thought it was as bonkers as her hubby and chuckled to herself at the very thought of it. God said that nothing was too hard for Him and that when He came back in nine months' time what He had promised would have come true.

To drop in on Abraham and Sarah nine months later, head for Bible book Genesis, chapter 21 and look at verses 1 to 3.

# NIGHT FIGHT

Jacob was the son of Isaac, who was the longed-for son of Abraham and Sarah. Jacob had been away from home for a few years but he was finally heading back to the land of his birth. He'd originally left to escape the wrath of his big brother (Esau), whom he'd double-crossed. Now it was his Uncle Laban he was running from.

God had hand-picked Jacob to head up a special nation of people who would show others who God was and how much He loved them. Couldn't God have found somebody better than Jacob? I suppose He could have done – but God specialises in taking ordinary people and making them extraordinary. Jacob knew he'd messed up, but he still wanted to trust God and do whatever God wanted. God was about to give our main man a second chance. Before Jacob reached home, he needed time out with God to work a few things through.

In the dead of night, as Jacob was all alone, a man appeared as if from nowhere. Was he an angel from God or was this God Himself? Whoever he was, he started wrestling with Jacob. Jacob wasn't having any of that – and fought back.

The two of them wrestled right through the night. What was going on? As the night wore on and the fight continued, Jacob became even more determined. He'd had enough of living on his wits. He figured it was time to live life God's way, and to do that he needed God's blessing. He wasn't going to let go of this guy, whoever he was, until he got it. As they tussled and tugged, the man from God asked a strange question. He asked Jacob what his name was. He then told Jacob that because he'd fought well and won, he was going to have a new name. It was 'Goodbye, Jacob' and 'Hello, Israel'. Jacob's life would never be the same again – he had received a new name, a blesssing and a limp.

To discover how Jacob got his limp, you'll need to find Bible book Genesis, chapter 32, verse 25 and then verses 30 through to 32.

# GO JOE!

You may have already heard the story about Joseph and his splendid coloured coat. Joseph was the apple of his dad's eye, which didn't go down too well with the rest of his brothers (all 11 of them). They'd had enough of Joseph the blue-eyed boy and his dreams of one day ruling over them. Joseph needed pulling down a peg or two and it was time he got his comeuppance.

The brothers were out and about looking after their dad's flocks. Jacob (their dad) dispatched Joe to go and check that they were getting on all right. As Joseph approached them they hatched a plot to kill him, throw his body into a well and make out it had been the work of wild animals.

Isn't brotherly love a wonderful thing?!

Reuben (the eldest) wasn't so keen on the plan and tried to save Joe's life by suggesting that they leave out the killing bit and just throw him down a well. (Reuben's idea was to rescue Joseph later.) Yep, they could run with that, or at least that's what they said to Reuben.

When Joseph arrived, they ripped off the long-sleeved, coloured coat his dad had made for him and flung their upstart brother into the well (which, fortunately for Joe, was dry at the time). With the dirty deed done, they put their feet up and tucked into their packed lunch.

Very soon a bunch of Ishmaelite traders passed by on their way to Egypt. One of the brothers (Judah) began to have second thoughts about killing Joseph. He had a better idea. How about selling him as a slave to the Ishmaelites? If they took Joseph to far away Egypt he'd be out of their hair forever.

So that's what they did. The brothers sold him for 20 pieces of silver and then went back to their dad and spun a gory yarn about what had befallen their poor brother, Joe.

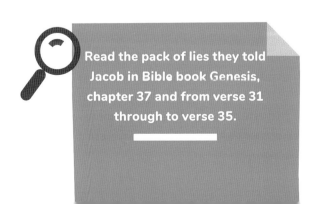

Read the pack of lies they told Jacob in Bible book Genesis, chapter 37 and from verse 31 through to verse 35.

I'll bet you've heard of a guy called Moses, haven't you? Although a Hebrew slave by birth, he'd been adopted by an Egyptian princess and brought up in Egypt's royal household. That's what I call jammy! But don't think that's the end of this story. There's more drama to come.

The Egyptian king (Pharaoh) was giving his Hebrew slaves a hard time and Moses was having none of it and ended up killing an Egyptian in the process. Oops!

When Pharaoh heard of this he wanted Moses' guts for garters. Realising his days of luxury were over, Moses did a runner as fast as his legs would carry him. So much for using his position of influence to rescue his people from slavery it looked like he'd well and truly blown it.

Moses ended up in the back of beyond in the land of Midian. Hopefully Pharaoh wouldn't find him there in the middle of the desert. He had little choice but to settle down and make the best of a bad job. Moses married a gal called Zipporah and spent his days tending the flocks of his father-in-law, Jethro.

Moses had been 40 when he'd scarpered from Egypt and now he'd hit the ripe old age of 80. Just when Moses had probably given up all hope of being part of God's rescue plan for the Hebrews in Egypt, God showed up.

Moses had been out with the flocks when God appeared to him in a rather odd way. A bush seemed to be on fire and from it came a voice, which was God's. Now that is dramatic! The bottom line is that God was giving Moses a second chance to finish what he'd started all those years ago.

Second time around though Moses wasn't quite so keen on the idea. I mean, how was one old man like him going to persuade Egypt's powerful Pharaoh to loosen his iron grip on his Hebrew slaves and let them go free? Come to think of it, what would the Hebrews think of Moses? What was going to persuade them that he was God's man for the moment?

Fear not! God had thought this one through.

You can find out how in Bible book Exodus, chapter 4 and verses 1 to 8.

# NIGHT STRIKE

Moses had tried just about everything he could to persuade Pharaoh to obey God and set his Israelite slaves free, but Egypt's king was having none of it. God had sent one plague after another to show Pharaoh who was boss but nothing doing. Pharaoh wasn't gonna budge.

In the end, God was left with no alternative but to inflict one final plague on the Egyptians. He was planning to strike dead every oldest son and every first-born creature in Egypt. Maybe then stubborn Pharaoh would realise that you don't mess with God.

But first things first: God had some important instructions to give the Hebrews to make sure that they weren't touched by His punishment. They were told that when God gave them the go-ahead, they should take the blood from a lamb or a young goat and paint it all around their front doors. The meat was then to be eaten as part of a special meal that would help the Israelites remember what God was going to do for them. There were other things, too, that God told the Israelites to do during the build up to the time when He was going to set them free. Finally the big day arrived and the Israelites shut themselves indoors and waited for Him to do His stuff.

At around midnight God showed up. He passed right over the Hebrew homes where the door-frames were coloured with blood.

Did God's final plague do the trick or did Pharaoh dig his stubborn heels in even further? Find out in Bible book Exodus, chapter 12 and verse 31.

# GOD'S TOP TEN

Everywhere you look there seem to be lists of the top ten this or the top ten that. It's one way of finding out what's popular and what matters most to us. Sometimes it's for fun and other times it's a lot more serious. The Bible has a 'top ten' list that is definitely not just for fun and which God most certainly intended people to take seriously.

If you haven't guessed already, I'm talking about the Ten Commandments. Let me tell you about them. The Israelites had been chosen by God to be His special nation. Their job was to show all the other nations what God was like. It wasn't that easy and, try as they might, the Israelites kept making a hash of things. What the Israelites really needed were some helpful guidelines to show them the things they *should* be doing and the things they *shouldn't*. With a few handy rules in place, doing things God's way ought to be a breeze. So God invited Moses (the leader of the Israelites) up to the top of a mountain to give him these Ten Commandments.

There were no iPads or Post-It Notes® for God to jot them down on in those days, so God settled for two stone slabs and had these rules carved onto them. Did these top ten do's and don'ts make living God's way easy peasy? Nope! But God had known that all along. First off, God simply wanted the Israelites to know what mattered to Him the most. God's long-term plan was that one day people would have such a good relationship with Him, they'd live according to these rules without even trying. For now, though, it would have to be a case of them *choosing* to live God's way.

To discover what was top of God's top ten, take a look in Bible book Exodus, chapter 20 and verses 1 to 3.

# BEZ IS THE BEST

Did you know that God likes camping?! Well, He does! In Bible book Exodus you'll find loads of stuff about a very special tent that God instructed the Israelites to build, just for Him.

Here's a bit of the background to the story. The Israelites were on their way to a land that God had given them to live in. The journey should have taken them a couple of weeks, but it ended up taking them 40 years (but that's another story).

Because the Israelites were always on the move, they lived in tents – which were easy to set up and easy to take down. The Israelites were God's special nation, so wherever they went, He went.

One day, God told their leader, Moses, that He wanted to live among them. Wow! What an awesome privilege. But hang on a minute… Surely God wasn't planning to live in one of the Israelite tents, was He?! No, He most certainly wasn't. God had something a little grander in mind.

The tent that God told Moses to build would be the most magnificent tent imaginable. It was called the Tabernacle, and measured 45 feet (that's nearly 14 metres) by 15 feet (roughly four and a half metres).

Not only did God give Moses detailed instructions about what the tent and the furnishings should look like, but He handpicked the guy who was to head up the whole thing.

His name was Bezalel, and God had given this guy wisdom and skill to work with gold, silver, bronze, stone and wood. Everything in the Tabernacle had to be tip-top quality, and Bezalel was the man to make sure that happened. Although Bezalel was a good craftsman already, God made him an absolutely brilliant one so that the Tabernacle would be a tent fit for God.

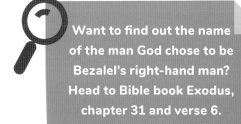

Want to find out the name of the man God chose to be Bezalel's right-hand man? Head to Bible book Exodus, chapter 31 and verse 6.

# GIVE IT UP
# FOR GOD!

There's loads of stuff in the Bible about making sacrifices to God, and sometimes it seems a bit hard to get your head round. Before the Israelite nation had a land of their own to settle in they wandered round the desert, setting up camp for a bit until it was time to move on again. Wherever they went, a big tent called the Tabernacle travelled with them. It was here that Israel's leaders met with God and it was here that sacrifices were made to Him.

All sorts of different sacrifices were made. A perfect whole animal was burnt to make up for their shortcomings. An offering of flour, baked cakes or grain was given as a way of making sure God saw the giver in a good light. The fat of an animal was burnt to keep God as your friend and the blood of an animal was sprinkled over the Tabernacle to show that everything bad had been removed.

The job of looking after all these sacrifices was left to a bunch of guys called priests. It certainly couldn't be done by any old Tom, Dick or Harry. Everything had to be done in a very particular way, just as God had told them. This was really important. One wrong move and the sacrifice was as good as useless in God's eyes. One of the more famous priests was none other than Moses' big bro, Aaron, and his first sacrifice was a nerve-wracking business. God warned him (and his sons who were helping) that if they put a foot wrong they'd be toast. Gulp! With great fear and trepidation they followed God's instructions to the letter. At long last their first sacrifice was done and they were still alive. What a relief!

That's when the weirdest of things happened...

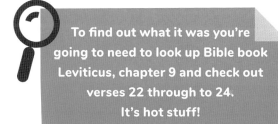

To find out what it was you're going to need to look up Bible book Leviticus, chapter 9 and check out verses 22 through to 24.
It's hot stuff!

# SCAREDY SCOUTS

If you think spies are a modern invention then think again. The Israelites were getting all geared up to enter the land of Canaan, which God had given them to conquer and settle in. First, in order to check out what the place was like and what sort of opposition they were likely to face, 12 spies were dispatched.

For 40 days the daring dozen darted about eyeing up Canaan. When they finally returned, the spies reported to Moses (the leader of the Israelites) what they'd seen. On the plus side, the land was brilliant for growing things, and to prove it they'd brought back a humungous bunch of grapes, which had to be carried by two of them. The downside was that the inhabitants of Canaan were powerful people who lived in fortified cities. It didn't stop there. Just to make matters worse, there were giants living in the land. Gulp! That soon put the wind up the Israelites. No way were they going to invade Canaan if that's what they were up against.

Caleb (one of the 12 spies) wasn't having any of the other Israelites's cowardly nonsense. He figured that if God had given them the land, a few giants or some fortified cities weren't gonna stop 'em. But, with the exception of Caleb and another spy called Joshua, the rest of the spies were planning to go nowhere.

Fear and panic quickly spread like wildfire through the Israelite camp. God was well cheesed off with the Israelites for not putting their trust in Him. If they didn't want to take possession of the land that He was giving them, then all the moaners and complainers would die in the desert where they were living.

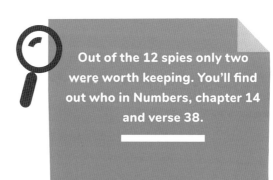

Out of the 12 spies only two were worth keeping. You'll find out who in Numbers, chapter 14 and verse 38.

# SILLY SIHON

In this Bible story we catch up with the Israelites as they are aimlessly roaming around in the desert. By now they should have been in the land of Canaan, which God had given them to settle down in, but they'd foolishly chosen not to enter it for fear of the inhabitants. God wasn't particularly happy about their bad decision and made it clear that they'd now have to wait until all the disobedient cowards had died before they got a second chance.

Wandering in the wilderness is not much fun when you've only got tents to live in and can't grow your own food to eat. Fortunately for the Israelites, God kindly provided them with food.

As they roamed from place to place the Israelites passed through lands ruled by various tribes and kings. Chances are that the inhabitants of these lands weren't too happy to have the vast Israelite nation on their doorstep and sometimes they let 'em know it. King Arad (a Canaanite king) had already attacked them along the way, although the Israelites got their own back.

Now the Israelites found themselves sandwiched between the land of the Amorites and the land of the Moabites. If they could just pass through without any fuss, that would be great.

Out of courtesy the Israelites sent messengers to King Sihon (the Amorite king) to ask if this was OK with him. Their plan was to travel on what was called 'the King's Highway' and they promised not to help themselves to any of the Amorites' crops or water en route. Seemed like a fair request.

Silly Sihon didn't think so. Why do I call him silly? Well, if he knew anything about the Israelites he'd know that God was with them. This meant that if anyone attacked God's special nation then God would defend them. King Arad had already discovered this to his cost and now King Sihon was about to make the same barmy botch-up as well.

Sure enough Sihon mustered his troops and launched all-out war against the Israelites. God tells Moses what he should not do next. What was it?

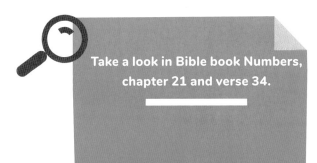

Take a look in Bible book Numbers, chapter 21 and verse 34.

# NO BRAINER

God gave the Israelites (His special nation) a simple choice to make. This wasn't something trivial like 'Shall I have custard with my salad?' or 'Do I wear one sock today or two?' – the choice that the Israelites had to make was a matter of life and death.

Here's the deal. God says there's a right way to live and there's a wrong way to live. If people do things God's way and everything will be hunky-dory (fine). If they do things any old way they want it will be bad news. Just like there are rules that they need to obey when crossing the road (to keep them safe from speeding camels), so there are rules that God has made to make sure all goes well.

God's rules were all about obeying Him. The reason obeying God was so important is that at the beginning of time the

world's first man and woman (Adam and Eve) disobeyed God and, as a result, lost His blessing on their lives. God's blessing is simply God looking after them and providing them with everything they need.

God is a good God and He'd hand-picked the Israelites to show the rest of the world what a loving God He is. Once He'd got them back on board, the way would be open for everyone else.

Here's a flavour of some of the blessings that were on offer for obeying God: their women would have no problems having kids and their animals would multiply; at harvest time their barns would be stacked to the rafters; they'd have God's protection from enemy attack; and whatever they set their hands to would be successful. In fact, God promised that every area of their lives would be blessed. Wherever they went and whatever they did, it would go well for them. Sounds too good to be true but it was there for the taking.

The flip-side of this was that if they chose to do their own thing and ignore God, the Israelites wouldn't just miss out on all these goodies, the complete opposite would happen and everything would go belly up. Put it like that and they'd have been barmy not to obey God. And, just in case they were barmy enough to think about not doing things God's way, He had some handy advice for them.

**Check it out in Bible book
Deuteronomy, chapter 30
and verses 19 and 20.**

# JUMPED-UP JOSHUA?

Poor old Moses. He'd led the Israelites out of slavery in Egypt, he'd stuck with them for 40 years in the desert after they'd rebelled against God, and now God wasn't going to let him lead them into the land of Canaan, which He'd given them as a place to settle in.

To be fair to God, it was Moses' fault. When the Israelites were grumbling about how thirsty they were and God told Moses to speak to a rock to release water, Moses whacked it twice because he was cheesed off with their moaning. For God's part, He was upset that Moses had not done what He'd commanded. The price for his disobedience was God not allowing him to enter Canaan. On the plus side, God did let Moses go up on a mountain to take a peek at the land before he died.

With Moses having to let go of the reins of leading the Israelites, they needed a new man at the helm to lead them into God's Promised Land. This was no time for putting a 'situation vacant' ad in the paper and doing job interviews. God already knew who He'd lined up to step into Moses' shoes (or perhaps I should say, sandals). The only guy in the frame, as far as God was concerned, was a fella called Joshua.

Who knows if the Israelites wondered how Joshua had managed to get into God's good books and land the top job in the land? God certainly did though, and to His way of thinking, Israel's new leader most certainly wasn't a jumped-up Joshua.

Joshua had lived through their nation's deliverance from slavery in Egypt. He'd been one of the 12 spies to spy out Canaan many years before, and he'd endured 40 years in the desert with his fellow Israelites who didn't agree with him that they should go and conquer the land then and there. Joshua had spent loads of his spare time in the tabernacle tent where he went to take time out with God and to worship Him. Plus, for many years Joshua had been acting as Moses' assistant.

So Joshua had learned from Moses and God all he needed to know about leading the Israelites and all about how to keep the Israelites on track with God.

Check out Bible book Numbers, chapter 27 and verses 18 to 23 to read the end of this story.

# ODD WAY OF DOING THINGS

God had given Joshua the job of leading the Israelites into the land of Canaan, which was going to be their new home. The only thing getting in the way was the River Jordan, but God soon sorted that by clearing a pathway through the water for them. So far, so good.

Now they were finally in Canaan all that was left was for everyone to find a patch of ground to live on and to settle down. Easy peasy. Er, not quite. There was just the small matter of the people who already lived in the land. They'd have to be got rid of first before anyone started building homes and planting flower beds. As if that wasn't enough, many of the towns and cities were surrounded by whopping great walls to prevent intruders (like the Israelites) from getting in.

The first of these cities was a place called Jericho. Before they'd had a chance to scratch their heads and to ponder how on earth they were going to conquer it, God came to the rescue, but with an extremely odd strategy. They weren't to lift a finger for six whole days. No fighting. No attacking. Nothing. All God wanted them to do was to march in a long procession around the city walls, once a day, for six days. And that was it.

I wonder how they felt as they strolled round and round the city walls for six whole days in full view of the people of Jericho? If the inhabitants were getting complacent then they had another thing coming. Day seven was about to change everything.

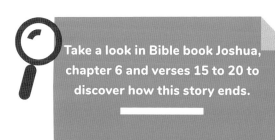

Take a look in Bible book Joshua, chapter 6 and verses 15 to 20 to discover how this story ends.

# NOT OVER THE HILL, YET!

Having successfully starting to conquer the land, we now catch up with Joshua as he begins to divvy it up (share) among Israel's 12 tribes. We're not going to go into detail about who got what but take it from me that the land was divided up between them and the Israelites finally had a land, which they could call their own.

One chap who keen to put down roots in Canaan was Caleb. He'd been one of the 12 spies Moses had sent to investigate Canaan 45 years earlier. Only Caleb and Joshua had come back with a report that it was theirs for the taking.

They'd taken God at his word when He'd promised the Israelites Canaan as their permanent home.

The trouble was that the other spies had taken their eyes off God (and forgotten that they were supposed to be trusting Him to give them victory), and instead were totally focused on how big and frightening the inhabitants of Canaan were.

The other ten spies were scared silly that they'd all be killed and recommended giving it a miss (which the Israelites did).

Caleb had waited long enough for the patch of land Moses had promised him. 'I am still as strong today as the day Moses sent me out; I'm just as vigorous to go out to battle now as I was then. Now give me this hill country that the Lord promised me that day,' said Caleb to Joshua.

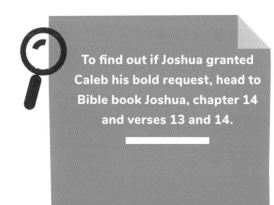

To find out if Joshua granted Caleb his bold request, head to Bible book Joshua, chapter 14 and verses 13 and 14.

# HELP, GOD!

What do you think of when you read the word 'judge'? I'll bet you're thinking of someone with a white wig, a black cloak and holding a little wooden mallet. Thought so. Well, the sort of judges who pop up in our next Bible story weren't anything like that. Joshua, Israel's leader, had died and in his place God appointed leaders who the Bible calls judges. With Joshua gone, the Israelites soon forgot about the God who had rescued them from slavery in Egypt and who had given them the land of Canaan in which to live. God was none too pleased with their rejection of Him and removed His hand of protection from them.

The king of Aram seized the opportunity, attacked the Israelites and conquered them. After eight terrible years of suffering under the king's hand the Israelites finally came to their senses and called out to God for help. They realised that they did need Him after all.

Did God ignore their cries? Of course He didn't. God had made a promise to be the God of the Israelites, so when they turned back to Him, He turned back to them. How did God rescue them? He raised up a guy called Othniel, Caleb's nephew, who beat the king of Aram and set them free. Did it all end happily for Israel? Well, yes and no.

While Othniel led the nation it enjoyed a time of peace. But guess what. No sooner had he died than the Israelites once again turned their back on God. This cycle of the Israelites rejecting God and Him then sending a judge to rescue them (when they cried out for help) happened seven times in total and involved 12 judges.

You can find out who the very last of Israel's judges was by reading Bible book Judges and the whole of chapter 13. Go on, give it a go!

# DARING DEB

In case you were wondering, Deborah and Barak weren't a husband and wife team like Adam and Eve. Deborah was one of the rulers of Israel and Barak was her military commander.

Like we said earlier, Israel's rulers at that time were called judges. The Israelites had finally settled in the land of Canaan after escaping from slavery in Egypt and these judges kept them on the right track with God and also led them into war against their enemies. All in all, there were at least 12 leaders whom the Bible calls judges. Deborah was judge number four and she'd come on the scene after Israel had been conquered by the Canaanite king, Jabin of Hazor.

Jabin had given the Israelites a hard time but it was their own fault. They'd turned their backs on God and as a result things had gone from bad to worse, ending up with 20 years of misery under this Canaanite king. The Israelites cried out to God and, being the kind God that He is, God came to the rescue, or rather He raised up Deborah to lead them to victory.

The feisty female judge summoned Barak and told him that God had given her a strategy to overthrow King Jabin. Barak was to take 10,000 fighting men to meet Sisera (Jabin's military commander) and trick him into coming out to fight. God promised that the Canaanite army would be defeated but Barak wouldn't go into battle without Deborah. Was he scared? Who knows? But because of this Deborah declared that he wasn't going to get any of the credit for winning the war. That would go to a woman. Did this really happen?

It isn't Deborah who wins the battle though – to find out which woman gets the credit have a look in Bible book Judges, chapter 5 and verse 24.

# WHAT ME?

The Midianites had been giving the Israelites a bit of a hard time, but only because God had allowed it. If only they'd stuck to worshipping Him and not the gods of the land they lived in, then everything would have been hunky-dory. God took pity on the Israelites when they begged Him for help and He raised up a leader to defeat their oppressors. Who did God pick for the job? None other than a rather insecure guy called Gideon.

Gideon was busily threshing wheat, when he had an unexpected visit from an angel who addressed him as 'brave and mighty man!' Come on! Get real! Anybody, especially God, would know that Gideon wasn't either of those things.

But the angel informed Gideon that he was God's choice to be the Israelites' main man to lead them to victory. Gideon must have thought that the angel was out of his mind. It was a crazy notion. How was someone puny like him going to rescue Israel? His clan was the weakest in the tribe of Manasseh and, to make matters worse, he was the least important member of his family. As far as Gideon was concerned, he was bottom of the pile. If this really was from God, Gideon was going to need some convincing.

Gideon needed some time to think, so he cooked the angel a tasty stew while he mulled things over. The angel nearly scared the pants off Gideon when he reached out and touched the bread and meat with his stick – and burned them to a cinder in an instant. Whoa! This really was God. Gideon was now fired up to lead his people to victory. With God as his strength, Gideon was ready for action. He blew the trumpet to call his troops to war. And then, at the eleventh hour, Gideon suddenly appeared to get cold feet. He needed to check this out one last time.

Take a look in Bible book Judges, chapter 6 and read verses 36 to 40 to discover Gideon's completely crazy idea to make absolutely sure that he was God's man for the job.

# SAM'S SECRET

Who's ever heard of a man getting his strength from having long hair? Muscles, yes, but long hair, never. Well Samson, the guy who features in this Bible story, certainly did. OK, so he was a bit of a beefy fella, but the secret of his strength really came from God. His mum had dedicated him to God from birth and vowed never to cut his hair as a sign that he belonged to God. For His part, God had Samson lined up to rescue His nation (Israel) from the pesky Philistines.

Samson had a soft spot for the ladies, and when he fell head over heels in love with Delilah (a Philistine gal), the Philistine kings saw their chance to get at Samson. They offered Delilah cartloads of cash if she could just find out what made Samson so strong. Double-crossing Delilah readily agreed but it took four attempts to get Samson to share his secret.

First off, he pretended that if he was tied up with seven brand-new bow strings he'd be a sitting duck for anyone who wanted to capture him. So that's what Delilah did. She had some Philistines waiting in the wings ready to nab Samson as soon as she'd tied him up. Just as they were about to seize Israel's hero he snapped the strings as if they were threads of cotton. Delilah played all coy and hurt and tried again.

Twice more Samson fooled Delilah with different answers and each time he freed himself. But Delilah wouldn't give up. She nagged and nagged until Samson cracked under the pressure and told her that it was all down to his hair. 'Cut my long hair', he told her, 'and I'd be as weak as the next man'.

To find out if Delilah got her cash, fast forward to Bible book Judges, chapter 16 and verses 18 through to 22.

# RA-RA-RUTH!

Naomi, her hubby Elimelech and their two boys had left Bethlehem (in the land of Judah) because of a famine, and ended up in Moab. Sadly, Elimelech died leaving Naomi and her kids all on their lonesome in a foreign land. The good news is that her boys (Mahlon and Chilion) ended up marrying a couple of local gals (Orpah and Ruth), but ten years down the line the poor chaps died as well.

Back in Judah the famine was over, and so Naomi decided that now was a good time to head back home to Bethlehem. She bid her fond farewells to her daughters-in-law and tried to persuade them that it was best if they didn't go with her.

Orpah and Naomi parted company but Ruth had other ideas. Wherever her mother-in-law went, she'd go. Naomi's people would be her people. Naomi's God would be her God. Naomi realised that Ruth had the bit between her teeth and wasn't going to take no for an answer, so the pair headed off for Bethlehem.

They arrived in Bethlehem just as the barley fields were being harvested. Ruth offered to collect up some of the grain that had been left by the harvest workers. In fact, it was part of God's Law for the Jewish people that they weren't allowed to reap up to the very edge of their fields at harvest time so that the poor and widowed would be able to gather food for themselves.

Of all the wild co-incidences, this particular field belonged to a rich relative of Naomi's called Boaz. The long and the short of it is that Naomi's loyal daughter-in-law ended up getting married to wealthy Boaz (nice one, Ruth!), but her story does not end there.

**Check out Bible book Matthew, chapter 1 and verses 5 and 6 to find out whose great-grandmother she ended up becoming.**

# HELLO!
# IS ANYONE THERE?

Samuel's mum Hannah had been desperate for a child.
She promised God that if she had a son, his life would be
dedicated to Him. One time, when she was praying to God in
Jerusalem's Temple, Eli the priest gave her the news that she'd
been waiting for. God had heard her prayers and she was
going to have a son.

When the baby was born they named the lad Samuel (which
means God hears) and Hannah told her hubby Elkanah about
her promise to God. He had no choice but to allow his wife
to have her way. While he was still very young, Hannah took
Samuel to the Temple and handed him over to the care of Eli
the priest. Each year Hannah and Elkanah would visit Samuel

and take with them a little robe for him to wear as he served God in the Temple. God was kind to Hannah and gave her three more sons and two daughters to make up for allowing Samuel to serve Him.

All the while, Eli's sons (who also worked in the Temple) were up to no good. God had a message for Eli about his wayward sons and He chose young Sam to deliver it. Samuel was sleeping in the heart of the Temple when he was awoken by somebody calling to him. The lad raced off to Eli check out what he wanted. Eli was bemused. He hadn't said anything. So Samuel went back to bed. Once again, he heard a voice calling his name. If you hadn't guessed already, it was God, but Samuel had never heard God speaking to him before so he hadn't a clue what God sounded like. He headed off to Eli again but, just like before, Eli denied having anything to do with it. For the third time Samuel went back to bed and, surprise, surprise, he was woken up once more by someone calling to him. At last the penny dropped and Samuel twigged that it was none other than God speaking.

To read God's message, look up Bible book 1 Samuel, chapter 3 and verses 11 through 14.

# KING THING

Israel had been led by a mixed bag of men (and one woman) for a few hundred years, but the Israelites were now itching for a bit of a change. Their present leader was a guy called Samuel, who wasn't getting any younger. Added to which, Samuel's two sons, Joel and Abijah, weren't exactly lining themselves up to be worthy successors to their well-respected dad. They were a couple of rogues.

The people of Israel decided to take matters into their own hands. Why couldn't Israel have a king to rule over them like every other nation? As far as Samuel was concerned, this was a complete non starter. He wasn't happy with the idea one bit. Israel didn't need a king to rule them. That was God's job.

Samuel went away and prayed to God about it.

What was God's answer? He told him to give the Israelites what they wanted but there would be consequences. If it was a king they wanted, then give them a king. God reminded Samuel that they had always been a rebellious people – and rejecting God as their King was just more of the same. God also told Samuel to warn them that a king would make soldiers of their sons; their sons would end up ploughing the king's fields (not their own); their daughters would end up working for the king as perfumiers, cooks and bakers; he'd nab their best fields, vineyards and olive groves and give them to his officials; he'd take a tenth of their corn and grapes for his royal courtiers; he'd take their servants and their best cattle and donkeys; he'd take a tenth of their flocks; and to top it all they themselves would end up as the king's slaves.

As if that wasn't enough, God also said that when all this did actually happen and the Israelites realised what a big boo-boo they'd made, He wouldn't listen to their moans and groans. It would be tough luck!

**Did Israel get a king? Find out in Bible book 1 Samuel, chapter 8 and verses 21 and 22.**

# SAUL'S FALL

Israel's very first king was a chap called Saul. Having a king wasn't God's idea. It was the Israelites who wanted a king to rule over them so that they could be just like all the other nations around them. For God's part, He'd wanted Israel to be different from everyone else so that He could be the one to look after His special people. Having warned the Israelites that having a king wasn't the best of ideas, He let them have their way. King Saul looked every bit the regal ruler on the outside but actually he wasn't so good on the inside. To be fair to the guy he tried his best but, when push came to shove, Saul was more concerned about what other people thought about him than what God thought. And that was the beginning of his downfall.

Having been told by God to take his army to war against the

Amalekites, King Saul mustered over 200,000 fighting men and went off to battle. God wanted to teach the Amalekites a lesson that they'd never forget. Their ancestors had ambushed the Israelites centuries earlier (completely unprovoked) and now it was time for their comeuppance. God's orders to Saul were to wipe them out entirely. Even the sheep and cattle were to be destroyed. Nothing or no one was to remain alive. Couldn't be clearer. So off King Saul went with his army and attacked the Amalekites.

Just when it looked like everything was going to plan, the prophet Samuel received an urgent message from God. Of all the barmy things, Saul had not only spared the life of the Amalekite king (Agag) but had also allowed his soldiers to hold on to some of the sheep and cattle for themselves.

Samuel headed for Saul with a face like thunder. OK Saul, so what is this bleating of sheep and lowing of cattle that the prophet could hear? Could it be plunder of the sort that God had strictly forbidden? The king blurted out all manner of excuses for disobeying God but none of it was going to wash with seething Samuel. Eventually King Saul came clean and said that he'd been afraid of his soldiers and had given in to them (rather than obeying God).

Having told Saul that his days as king were numbered, Samuel had one last piece of unfinished business to do.

Find out what it was in Bible book 1 Samuel, chapter 15 and verses 32 to 35.

# DISCO DAVID

Some people have no problem enjoying a good old knees-up to celebrate a birthday or something like that but they get a wee bit uncomfortable when it comes to getting excited about God. Even more so, because it was God who first set an example. When God created the world it was He who made a point of saying that it was good, over and over again. God just loved people bigging things up and that's what this Bible story is about.

Israel's new king (David) had just got himself his very own royal city to live in (Jerusalem) and now he wanted to bring Israel's ark box there to stay. Just in case you didn't know, the ark was a golden box in which were kept two stone slabs. On them were engraved God's Ten Commandments to the

Israelites. The ark was carried using long poles, which were held by priests. The ark represented God being with them. This special box had travelled with the Israelites through much of their history and was very important to them.

Now that David was king, bringing the ark to Jerusalem was top of his list. He and his men set out to fetch it from a place called Baalah of Judah where it had been kept. It was loaded onto an ox cart and off they went. Everyone was having a high old time leaping, dancing and singing as the procession wended its way back to Jerusalem. Then disaster struck. One of the oxen lost its footing and a guy called Uzzah reached out to stop the ark from falling. Zap! God struck Uzzah down dead for not treating the ark with respect.

David decided to leave the ark at the house of Obed-Edom while he figured out what to do next. For the three months it was there, Obed-Edom revelled in God's blessings. So, when King David got wind of this, he decided to fetch the ark again. But, this time he made sure the ark was carried properly by the priests and not on any old cart. The king had learned his lesson.

Once again David and his entourage partied all the way back to Jerusalem. The king even took off his royal robes to celebrate. While God may have loved it, there was one person who thought that the king looked ridiculous.

**Find out who that was in Bible book 2 Samuel, chapter 6 and verses 16 to 23.**

# HERE TODAY...

There aren't that many characters from the Bible who have an expression named after them but here are a few: 'The patience of Job' (a guy who went through a bit of rough patch), 'As old as Methuselah' (he lived to a whopping 969 years old!) and 'The wisdom of Solomon' (Israel's third king). Solomon's dad (David) had reigned as Israel's king for 40 years and he was a tough act to follow. Solomon knew first-hand what it took to please the people but more importantly he knew what it took to please God.

Soon after he became king, God appeared to Solomon in a dream and told him to ask whatever he wanted and it was his.

Wow! There's an offer you can't refuse. Top of Solomon's list was wisdom.

God was as good as His word and gave the king the wisdom that he'd asked for. Not only that but God also made Solomon successful and rich in everything he did.

It proved to be the best decision that Solomon ever made. His wisdom helped him build a temple for God, a palace for himself, make the nation rich beyond anyone's wildest dreams and solve difficult dilemmas.

Sad to say Solomon's glory days didn't last. He became so rich and powerful that anything was his for the taking. This included wives, of which he had 700, and concubines (wives of less importance) of which he had 300. That makes a grand total of 1,000! The Bible says that it was his wives who were eventually his downfall. Why's that? Solomon made the bad mistake of paying more attention to the gods of some of his wives than to the God who had made him king in the first place. God wasn't pleased one little bit and told Solomon so. From then on things went from bad to worse. It seemed to Solomon that the good times were gone for good and all because he'd disobeyed God. Want to get a flavour of what was going through the downcast king's head?

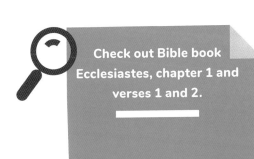

Check out Bible book Ecclesiastes, chapter 1 and verses 1 and 2.

# PAINFUL PARTING

Have you ever tried to do the splits with your legs? It's painful, isn't it? In the Bible story we're going to look at now, God's special nation was about to split and as you'll soon find out, it was jolly painful for them as well.

Israel's third king (Solomon) had started out really well and put God right at the very centre of things. Putting God first meant the nation prospered in a big way. Israel had gold and silver coming out of its ears (not literally of course) and all the nations around were amazed at what an awesome king Solomon was.

Not for long. Some people collect key rings and others collect seashells but King Solomon, well, he collected wives. Turn back a page to find out just how many he had! The king's wives weren't all from Israel so they didn't all worship Solomon's God. They brought with them gods of their own. God was having none of that and decided to put a stop to this wickedness.

God collared a chap called Jeroboam and gave him the heads-up that Solomon's days were numbered and that when the king had died, Israel would be divided in two. Jeroboam had fallen on his feet 'cos God said that he could be king of the top half of the divided nation. Not only that, but it would still be called Israel. Ten of Israel's tribes would form this new northern Israel and the tribe of Judah would be left on its own to form the new southern nation which would be called... well, it's probably pretty obvious what it would be called, isn't it? It was going to be called Judah. How original was that?

Want to know who took hold of the reins of Judah after Solomon's death? Of course you do.

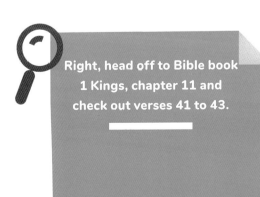

Right, head off to Bible book 1 Kings, chapter 11 and check out verses 41 to 43.

# SACRIFICE SIZZLER

Elijah the prophet had been in hiding for around about three years. Wicked King Ahab of Israel and his equally wicked wife (Jezebel) wanted him dead because he'd decreed a drought over the land. God now wanted Elijah to tell the king that He was going to send rain. King Ahab didn't exactly roll out the red carpet for God's prophet. He said that Elijah was the worst troublemaker in Israel. Elijah challenged the king to bring the 450 prophets of Baal and the 400 prophets of the goddess Asherah (whom Ahab's wife supported) to a place called Mount Carmel.

The event drew a big crowd and once everyone had assembled, Elijah threw down the gauntlet: 'Make up your minds. If the Lord is God, worship Him. If Baal is God, worship him.' Elijah had two bulls brought to him: one for him and one for the prophets of Baal. They cut their bulls into pieces, put them on an altar and stacked it up with firewood. 'Pray to your god and I will pray to mine, and the one who answers by sending fire, he's God,' announced Elijah.

Elijah let the prophets of Baal have first crack of the whip and they ended up making right old fools of themselves, dancing round their altar and yelling out to their god. The more frantic the prophets of Baal got, the more Elijah goaded them. It was pretty obvious that Baal wasn't going to come up with the goods. Elijah was beginning to enjoy this and started to taunt them that maybe their god had popped to the loo.

Next it was Elijah's turn. Elijah dug a trench around his altar, filled it full of water and then soaked the bull and the firewood until it was drenched. Elijah prayed to God that He would prove that He was Lord. Zap! Fire flamed down from heaven and burned the sacrifice to ashes, drying up the trench in the process.

How did the people react?
Have a look in Bible book
1 Kings, chapter 18 verse 39.

# TRANSPORT TALES

Have you ever been on a journey where you've had to change along the way? Perhaps you've had to change trains. Maybe you've gone from a taxi to an aeroplane. And when you were little there's every chance that you'd have been taken from your car and transferred to a child's buggy.

Well, fasten your seatbelts because this transport tale will beat 'em all. It stars a guy called Jonah who was a prophet of God. Jonah had a bit of a problem on his hands. Actually, he had a very big problem. The problem was this. God had given Jonah the job of telling the nasty Ninevites that He was giving them one last chance to quit being bad. If they didn't, God would call time on their wicked ways and get rid of the lot of 'em.

Jonah was more than happy to go along with the 'get rid of the lot of 'em' bit but he wasn't too keen on the 'giving them one last chance' bit. As far as jaded Jonah was concerned the rotten enemies of his nation deserved everything they had coming to them. No way did he want God to let them off the hook. So Jonah took a boat in the opposite direction and hoped that God wouldn't notice he'd scarpered. But God did.

God stirred up a stinking storm and when the sailors on the boat found out that Jonah was to blame they flung him overboard... and the storm subsided. Was that the end of the road (if the sea can have roads) for Jonah? Not yet! This was simply God's way of transferring the runaway prophet to a different means of transport and of getting him back on track. Which is why a ginormous fish swallowed Jonah whole and kept him stowed away for three dark days in its bilious belly.

Head for Bible book Jonah, chapter 2 and verse 10 and then keep going to chapter 3 and verses 1 to 10 for the rest of the fishy tale.

# CONNIVING KINGS

The nation of Israel had a falling out and split into two. One part kept the name Israel and made its capital in Samaria. The other part took the name Judah and kept Jerusalem as its main city. For the next few hundred years the two were sworn enemies and forever at each other throats. Along the way, most of the kings of Israel and Judah also drifted away from following the God who had started their nation (when it was united).

Often as not, Israel and Judah simply went their own way and kept God out of it. No wonder things were going from bad to worse.

It all came to a head when King Pekah was ruler of Israel and King Ahaz was ruler of Judah. Pekah sneakily joined forces with King Rezin of Aram (I hope you're keeping up with all these kings) to attack Jerusalem. The two armies marched up against the city and surrounded it. Ahaz stood his ground and held them off but he knew it would only be a matter of time before Jerusalem fell to his enemies. So, he concocted a cunning plan of his own. He sent messengers to say to Tiglath-Pileser king of Assyria (yes, yet another king!) to come and rescue him. In return he emptied Israel's coffers of all its silver and gold and offered it to the King of Assyria by way of payment. But that wasn't all. As if turning his back on God wasn't enough, King Ahaz also took all the silver and gold from Jerusalem's Temple and handed this over as well.

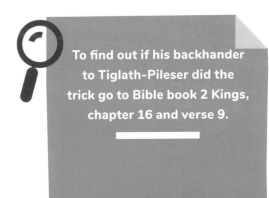

To find out if his backhander to Tiglath-Pileser did the trick go to Bible book 2 Kings, chapter 16 and verse 9.

# DAN IS NEARLY DIN-DINS

Here's a Bible story I'll bet you've heard. It's about a guy called Daniel who was captured by the Babylonians (along with just about everyone else from his homeland of Judah) and taken away to live in far off Babylon. Daniel was just a teenager when he was exiled to Babylon but because God was on his case, he swiftly rose through the ranks of the Babylonian royal household and eventually ended up just one step away from being the country's main man. And that's where we catch up with Daniel in this bit of the Bible.

The king of Babylon (Darius) had elevated our Dan to the position of president (along with two other guys), ruling over the land's 120 governors. All was not sweetness and light between Daniel and the governors (or, for that matter, his two fellow presidents). They didn't like this social-climbing outsider one little bit and set about plotting his downfall.

It was no secret that Daniel worshipped God so they tricked unsuspecting Darius into making it illegal to pray to anyone but their king for 30 days. Sneaky! Anyone caught disobeying this new law would be thrown into a den of lions. Did Daniel cave in to this devious decree? Nope! As bold as brass Daniel went home and prayed to God as if nothing had happened.

Daniel's enemies wasted no time in snitching him up to King Darius, who had no choice but to have his loyal servant arrested and flung into the lions' den. Darius was gutted that he'd been duped and he hoped that Daniel's God would protect him from becoming main course for those lunching lions. So, did Daniel turn into cat food or did God save him?

All the gory details are revealed in Bible book Daniel, chapter 6 and verses 19 through to 24.

# BYE-BYE BABYLON

This next Bible story happened a whopping 2,500-ish years ago and features an unlikely hero called Cyrus. Cyrus was in fact the king of Persia and as we dive into this story the Persians were still gloating over their recent conquest of the mahoosive Babylonian empire and turning it into one of their colonies. Nice work, Cyrus!

Living in Babylon at that time were also a bunch of people who'd rather not be there if they had the chance. These were the Jews and 70 years earlier, Nebuchadnezzar, king of Babylon had attacked their nation, destroyed its Temple in Jerusalem and taken them back to Babylon as captives.

To be fair, the Jewish people of that day had it coming to them. God had continually warned them to turn from their wicked ways but they chose to ignore His warnings. Not only had they rejected God but they'd taken to worshipping other gods in His place. Being exiled to Babylon was the punishment for that rebellion. Being a good God, He'd also set a time for them to return to Israel and that time had finally arrived.

Amazingly, God was going to use King Cyrus to restore the Jewish people to their homeland. Why do I say amazingly? Because Cyrus didn't actually worship the God of the Jewish people, but despite that, God put it on his heart to send the Jewish exiles back to Israel and to rebuild its Temple.

Cyrus even commanded his own people to provide the Jews with silver, gold, livestock and anything else they'd need for their return.

As if that wasn't enough, there was one more generous thing that King Cyrus did to ensure the returning Jews had a good send-off.

**To find out what that was, head to Bible book Ezra, chapter 1 and verses 7 to 11.**

# TEMPLE TIME

The Jewish people were finally heading back to Israel after their 70-year exile in Babylon. It was good to be back but there was much to be done before the place looked like home once again. The Babylonians had made a pretty good job of destroying the place before they left and there was plenty of rebuilding to do, including their Temple in Jerusalem.

The job of overseeing this fell to a guy called Zerubbabel who was one of their tribal leaders. His right-hand man was Joshua, the high priest and between them they set about making sure everything was done properly.

King Cyrus, who had made it possible for the Jews to return to Israel, had helpfully sent them off with their bags packed with silver and gold.

Some of this they used to pay the stonemasons and carpenters. God's temple had to be the best of the best and tip-top craftsmen came at a price.

They also gave drink and olive oil to the people of Sidon and Tyre so that they would ship cedar logs from Lebanon, something Cyrus king of Persia had authorised.

After just over one year of arriving back in Israel, work finally began on rebuilding the Temple and of putting God well and truly back at the heart of their nation.

As the builders laid the foundation of the Temple, the priests with trumpets and the Levites with cymbals launched into a song of praise to God. The rest of the Jews weren't going to be left out. This was a day to celebrate and together they gave a loud shout of praise to the God who had made it possible for them to return and to begin rebuilding the Temple.

Between you and me the occasion was all a bit too much for some of the Jews.

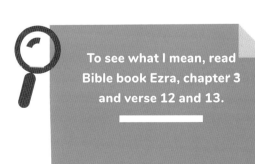

To see what I mean, read Bible book Ezra, chapter 3 and verse 12 and 13.

# ESTHER TO THE RESCUE

King Xerxes ruled over his vast empire from the city of Susa. Along the way he'd conquered and captured the Jewish nation. The king and his wife Queen Vashti had fallen out with each other and Xerxes thought it was about time he got himself another queen. He dispatched his servants to scour the land for a beautiful new bride to replace Vashti. All the young hopefuls were brought back to the palace and prepared for a meet-up with the king.

Xerxes eventually picked a girl called Esther to be his new queen. Esther was a Jew but she didn't let on to the king. One day, her uncle Mordecai overheard a plot to kill Xerxes, reported it and the would-be assassins were executed. Soon after this, a guy called Haman got promoted by King Xerxes, but much to Haman's annoyance Mordecai refused to bow down to him. Haman was well mad and hatched a plan to kill not only Mordecai (on a gallows) but all the Jews in the land.

Mordecai secretly visited Esther to warn her of what Haman was up to. It was time for Esther to blow her cover. Esther persuaded the king to have Haman invited to a special banquet. When the day arrived, Haman thought he'd hit the big time. A banquet specially for him. Wow!

That night, the king could not sleep so he had the official records read to him, which included how Mordecai had uncovered a plot to kill the king. The king called for Haman and asked him what should be done for a man the king wanted to honour. Thinking that he was referring to him, Haman suggested a regal procession on horseback through Susa. The king agreed to his idea but it was Mordecai who got the victory lap of the city and Haman was the one who ended up leading him round.

When it was all over Haman felt humiliated, but worse was still to come. Esther invited Haman back to the palace again and this time she snitched on him to the king, telling Xerxes all about the wicked plot to kill the Jewish people... and that included her!

The king was furious with Haman and if you want to find out the end to this story, head for Bible book Esther, chapter 7 and verse 10.

# MARRIAGE MESS

Around 80 years after the Jewish people had returned from exile in Babylon they had a surprise visit from a chap called Ezra. He was part of the Jewish community still living in Babylon and had been given permission by King Artaxerxes to go to Israel to see whether the Jews there were still being faithful to God, or not. Ezra was both a priest and a scholar, which meant he knew a thing or two about the Jewish Law and worshipping God.

   Artaxerxes was obviously in a generous mood and loaded up Ezra and his travelling companions (there were hundreds of people going with him) with just about everything they might need for the journey. When they finally rocked up in Jerusalem

(Israel's capital city) Ezra quickly discovered that all was not well with the Jews living there.

The priests and the people had almost completely ignored God's command not to marry anyone from the surrounding nations (for fear that they'd start worshipping their gods). Sure enough, this is exactly what had happened and it wasn't only God who was displeased with them. Ezra was also mortified and spent the next few days weeping before God at how his fellow Jews had turned from God's ways.

But all was not lost! Ezra's tears had made the Jews realise the error of their ways and before long they were blubbing tears of remorse along with him. Ezra knew that a few wet eyes wasn't enough and drastic action was needed. He ordered everyone to assemble in Jerusalem where he would then tell them how to put things right.

Want to know what that drastic action was? Of course you do.

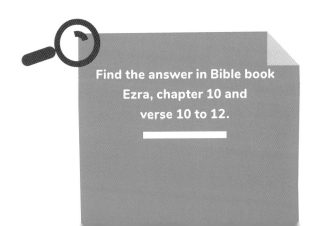

Find the answer in Bible book
Ezra, chapter 10 and
verse 10 to 12.

# THE REBUILDING GOES AHEAD

If you know anything about the Jewish people, you'll be well aware that Jerusalem (their capital city) was very special to them. Sad to say, Jerusalem had been destroyed by invaders and the inhabitants captured and taken to a foreign land.

One of the exiles (Nehemiah) had done well for himself and had ended up as a servant in the royal palace. News reached Nehemiah that his beloved Jerusalem's walls were falling down, so he summoned up all the courage he could muster and asked the king (Artaxerxes) if he'd let him go back to repair them. Amazingly, the king said 'Yes' to Nehemiah's request, and sent him on his way with an armed escort and made sure he had all the building materials to complete the task.

On his arrival in Jerusalem, Nehemiah soon realised that he had a big job on his hands. Jerusalem lay in ruins. Its gates had been burned and the walls were crumbling. With God's help Nehemiah set about turning things round. He rallied the support of every Jewish person he could find. Each family was given a job to do and nobody got away with doing nothing. From the richest to the poorest, everyone was expected to roll up their sleeves and muck in.

Just when things were getting under way, Sanballat, Tobiah and Geshem (enemies of the Jews) decided that they didn't like the idea of Jerusalem being rebuilt, and tried every dirty trick in the book to stop it. They spread rumours that the Jewish people were planning a revolt, they ridiculed Nehemiah's rebuilding plan and said it wouldn't work, and they even attempted to lure Nehemiah away to kill him – but the work went on. Nehemiah and his fellow Jews remained armed and alert. No way was anyone gonna stop them.

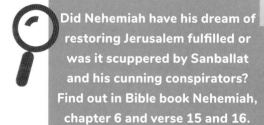

Did Nehemiah have his dream of restoring Jerusalem fulfilled or was it scuppered by Sanballat and his cunning conspirators? Find out in Bible book Nehemiah, chapter 6 and verse 15 and 16.

# BETTER LATE THAN NEVER!

Have you ever stood at a pedestrian crossing and wondered how much longer you've got to wait before you're allowed to cross the road? Well, imagine what it must have been like for the Israelites. God had promised that one day he'd send the Christ (Jesus) to rescue them, so in preparation they'd rebuilt Israel's Temple in Jerusalem.

In actual fact, Jesus didn't show up for around another 400 years, which is an awful lot of waiting if you ask me. So, why did God make them wait so long? Good question!

Well, although the Jewish people had returned to Israel (from their exile in Babylon), most of them hadn't really returned to the God who had started their nation.

Things had begun well enough with Nehemiah overseeing the work of rebuilding the Temple. But then things ground to a bit of halt. A guy called Zechariah eventually rocked up to chivvy them on and get things moving again. While he was at it he also reprimanded the Israelites for forgetting about God and going after the idols of the surrounding nations. Tut, tut!

It was all very well rebuilding the Temple but if they weren't going to worship the God whose Temple it was, then it was all for nothing. OK, so they did begin offering sacrifices to God and reintroducing His special feasts but, to be honest, they weren't really interested in God Himself, just the rituals.

If they'd returned to God with all their heart, who knows if Jesus would have come sooner. But something we do know is what a prophet called Malachi had to say to the Israelites to encourage their descendants that Jesus would indeed one day finally show up.

You can check it out in
Bible book Malachi, chapter 3
and verse 1.